PASSIVE INCOME STREAMS

10 HIGHLY PROFITABLE SOURCES

DIVERSIFY YOUR INCOME: MAKE MONEY WORK FOR YOU ANDBECOME FINANCIALLY FREE

JONATHAN S. WALKER

Copyright © 2017 JONATHAN S. WALKER

All rights reserved.

DEDICATION

This Book Is Dedicated To All Who Desire To Be Financially Free. May Your Efforts Bear Fruits In the Near Future And I Wish You All The Success In Life.

&

I dedicate this book as well to my two beautiful children and my loving wife who have been nothing short of being my light and joy throughout the years.

CONTENTS

Introduction: Passive Income—A Future of Financial Freedom

Chapter 1: 10 Popular Sources of Passive Income

Chapter 2: A Pipeline of eBooks, Apps & Blogs

Chapter 3: Real Estate Returns

Chapter 4: Investing in Stocks, Bonds & Annuities

Chapter 5: Building/Buying Websites & Domains

Chapter 6: Monitor & Adjust Your Sources

Conclusion:

⚓ Copyright 2017 by Diana Watson - All rights reserved.

The following eBook is reproduced below with the goal of providing information that is as accurate and reliable as possible. Regardless, purchasing this eBook can be seen as consent to the fact that both the publisher and the author of this book are in no way experts on the topics discussed within and that any recommendations or suggestions that are made herein are for entertainment purposes only. Professionals should be consulted as needed prior to undertaking any of the action endorsed herein.

This declaration is deemed fair and valid by both the American Bar Association and the Committee of Publishers Association and is legally binding throughout the United States.

Furthermore, the transmission, duplication or reproduction of any of the following work including specific information will be considered an illegal act irrespective of if it is done electronically or in print. This extends to creating a secondary or tertiary copy of the work or a recorded copy and is only allowed with express written consent from the Publisher. All additional right reserved.

The information in the following pages is broadly considered to be a truthful and accurate account of facts and as such any inattention, use or misuse of the information in question by the reader will render any resulting actions solely under their purview. There are no scenarios in which the publisher or the original author of this work can be in any fashion deemed liable for any hardship or damages that may befall them after undertaking information described herein.

Additionally, the information in the following pages is intended only for informational purposes and should thus be thought of as universal. As befitting its nature, it is presented without assurance regarding its prolonged validity or interim quality. Trademarks that are mentioned are done without written consent and can in no way be considered an endorsement from the trademark holder.

INTRODUCTION
PASSIVE INCOME—A FUTURE OF FINANCIAL FREEDOM

You've just come home from a beautiful week spent on the beach, or an active adventure vacation spent hiking, exploring and letting your imaginations run free, and now it's time to return to the real world. If you're letting passive income work for you while you were away, you're not dreading coming home to a stack of bills and a diminished bank account.

Instead, you can't wait to come back and check your accounts to see how much money you made during your time away. Sound like a fantasy? It doesn't have to be. That's what passive income is all about—it should work harder than you do.

Don't let anyone blow smoke up your behind when it comes to enjoying all the financial freedom that having several streams of passive income can create for you. Let me clarify a few very important points about the realities of passive income. First of all, creating avenues of passive income isn't a "get rich quick" trendy scheme that requires no work on your part. In fact, developing diverse pathways of passive income can be quite challenging and isn't very passive in the beginning.

Sorry for being a buzzkill, but to understand the actual advantages that building significant passive income can provide, it's necessary that you, perhaps, change your perspective. Look at our title to this book. You may have missed one vital word—future. To build passive income takes an investment of time and money upfront. To create financial freedom down the road, you need to be willing to do what others refuse to do—work harder, save, and invest your extra money in building a future that makes that fantasy scenario we started with reality.

To better understand what passive income is, let's examine what it is not. Passive income is not a second or part-time job. After all, that would just be creating more of what you already have, right? If you are working a 9-5 job, trading time for money, you are limited to the amount of money you can make. There is only so many hours in a day—only so much time you can devote to making more money, whether that is overtime or another part-time job to supplement your regular income. This is known as "active" income.

Passive income follows a whole different set of rules than active income. Once you have discovered the passive income avenues you wish to pursue, and once you have made your initial investment of time and money, then real passive income continues to work for you while you move on to something else. You can and should have many avenues of passive income, track them frequently, and determine which ones generate the highest and most consistent returns. It's different for everyone. One of the most incredible differences between active and passive income is the surprising amount of money you can generate. What you have to look forward to is that eventually, you'll be putting very little effort into maintaining the source of that income. The truth is, passive income is only limited by your imagination.

For those of you who feel more secure with a definition—passive income is the money earned that continues to roll in with very little to no effort required after your initial upfront investment of time and money. A stream of passive income is when your focus moves from one source to many sources, to diversify your efforts and increase your successful returns, even if one or two streams are not currently producing the results you expected.

What Can Passive Income Do for You?

We've already determined your passive income is going to work for your "future" financial freedom, so it's necessary not to expect instant gratification, right? Wrong! Once you begin seeing the results of your passive income streams working on your behalf, you'll feel gratified seeing your money multiply. What you'll learn are ways to manage and control your future that you never thought yourself capable of doing. One success will build upon another until your confidence, and increased feelings of self-worth will be almost as rewarding as the additional income you are generating. Here are some of the things you can expect when you have created several successful streams of passive income.

- You have the freedom to work on what you feel passionate about rather than being trapped by a 9-5 job with limited monetary gain and even less personal gratification.
- You can plan to retire early, explore magnificent world class destinations that you may never have had the opportunity to do without your passive income.
- You can spend more time with your family and not continue to be a slave to your job.

- You can help others and volunteer for heartfelt causes.
- You can live a healthier, stress-free life.
- You can let your imagination and creative spirit run wild—writing the next best seller, painting on the beach, or exploring faraway lands and people.
- Bottom line—you can live the life of those you currently envy!

Sounds Good—But Where Do You Start?

I would love to say that you have already started by reading this book, but I'd be remiss if I didn't explain a sad fact. Many people read about creating passive income, and that is all the further they get to achieving it. Either they think they don't have the skills or knowledge, or they lack the motivation to do what it takes today to plan for a better tomorrow. Don't be one of those people. Every new endeavor comes with an initial energy and inner spark that excites and inspires you. Unfortunately, if that initial spark isn't attended to, it will not grow into a raging fire that spurs you to continue to work all the avenues of passive income that could create financial freedom. The enthusiasm you may be feeling as you read these pages needs to be protected and nurtured—worked into a viable fuel that speeds your progress. It's not only important to know how to start, but you must know how to push yourself through some of the more demanding up-front challenges of creating passive income. You must be "active" in your pursuit of "passive" income.

Here are three tips to help you get a good start in building a stream of passive income.

1. Ask yourself why you want to do this? Are you only in it for the money, or would you like to do something for which you feel passion? Very important question. Many of the streams of

passive income you will be interested in pursuing will require passionately presenting your ideas to others. People can spot a "huckster' a mile away, so whatever you choose to do, make it something you believe in and enjoy. Don't just make it an idea or product you need to push off on people to make money.

2. If you don't have much money to invest in the beginning, that's okay. However, count on spending a good deal of time in planning and preparing to take your product or service to market and make it a success. Take the time to consider your consumer, to understand their needs and wants so that you make sure your choice will be beneficial and long-lasting. If you are working a full-time job while you're getting your passive income going, know that you may not have a lot of time to be a Sunday

afternoon couch potato anymore.

3. Realize that there is no such thing as passive income that is 100% passive, no matter how much planning and preparation you have given it. Even investments in stocks require you to check on the market and frequently buy and sell to optimize your investment. If you've chosen eBooks, blogs, websites, or apps, you still need to continue to produce, so you have a pipeline of possibilities. Though maintenance may be minimal as your passive income matures, you'll still want to devote time to new endeavors. If you are passionate about what you are doing, you'll enjoy the process as much as the end results (1).

Some passive income streams require a substantial amount of money to start. If those are the types of passive income that flip your switch, you'll need to save some money first. For example, if real estate or stocks are what interests you, then you have two way to begin. Either you win the lottery or inherit, or you do it the old-fashioned way and save. Instead of having a Christmas or vacation fund, you may want to start a passive income fund. Save a little out of your check each month and sock it away. Consider cleaning out your garage and having a large yard sale. Take the proceeds from the sale, and begin investing just a little to get your feet wet. Once you experience some success, you can take your profit and reinvest, building and diversify your investments.

That word "diversify" is crucial when it comes to planning what type of passive incomes to choose. There is wisdom in the adage, "Don't put all your eggs in one basket." If you have several different things working for you, when demand is down for one, it may be up for another. Plus, who wants to do the same thing over and over, when you could be enjoying exploring different things every day? Leave that for your 9-5 job. Speaking of which, the earlier you can begin building an ongoing stream of passive income, the better. Waiting until you retire to decide whether you'll have enough money to retire comfortably, is like leaving your car windows rolled down in a rain storm and worrying if your seats will get wet. Of course, they will!

Sure, if you're retired, you'll have all the time in the world to invest in building passive income—but, no money. Even the smallest of ventures usually requires some monetary investment. Waiting until you're older to think about your future is never a good idea.

So, where and when do you start? There's no time

like right now. Here are five easy steps to get started on building a steady stream of passive income.

Step #1:

Make a list of things you love to do. Include hobbies, unique talents you possess, creative outlets you have, or perhaps objects you have collected over the years.

Step #2:

Write down what you feel would be a comfortable and believable amount of money for you to make in a year's time with your stream of passive income.

Step #3:

Now compare the two steps, looking at what you could do that would contribute to your goal. For example: If your goal was to make $10,000 per year in passive income, what's on that list in step #1 to help you do that? Is there anything that would appeal to a significant number of people if you were to market that product or service? Let's say your hobby was to play the piano. Could you write an eBook on how to play the piano? Could you have an online course, teaching beginners how to play? Could you have YouTube lessons that would complement your book, demonstrating a step-by-step course? Could you have a website offering several beginner books or beginner sheet music for sale that would best help the beginner? Could you hold a webinar to teach several enrollees to play at once, charging a reasonable fee, of course?

Once you've given full reign to your imagination, the list of possible products and services are endless. The key is to let your mind run with wild abandon to all the possibilities. Make sure you write them all down, no matter how silly they might sound. Somewhere inside the silliness might just be an amazing way to earn passive income.

Step #4:

Start small. If you need inventory for your passive income, don't buy a warehouse full and then pay to have it stored—test the waters. In case this particular type of passive income was not successful, you don't want to lose too much on a fail. There will be some things in which you invest time and money, which go anywhere. Don't get discouraged. All it could mean is that you need to do a better job of planning and preparing before investing the time and money.

Step #5:

Involve a well-wisher. What I mean by this is, solicit the support of someone who cares about your success. If it's a close family member, make sure they will benefit from the sacrifices they will be asked to make as well. For instance, if you are investing your previously free time or some of your family time to work on your own ventures, then an involved spouse will be less likely to burden you with complaints. Share your goals and get that person aboard right from the get go so their participation can help minimize your time investment.

Most importantly, believe in pursuing passive. If you have things on your list that you like but don't believe anybody else would, it's probably not going to be an excellent addition to your stream of passive income. It might be better to postpone that one until you have some successes under your belt. Early success is excellent inspiration for continued activity. Even though your ideas may be out of the norm, that's the great thing about passive income. Nothing's off limits. If your idea sounds too far out there, find an expert that you respect in the field of your interest, and let that expert help you get grounded. Who knows, with just a little help your idea could go from far out to far-reaching, attracting others to your cause or venture.

With expectations intact, now give all these things some thought and continue reading to see some specifics on how to make your passive income prosperous.

CHAPTER 1: 10 POPULAR SOURCES OF PASSIVE INCOME

Almost anything can become a source of passive income, so what you choose to include in your stream should be what excites you—what you feel passionate about so that you can enjoy the journey of building a financially free future. Learn to think about passive income differently. It's not a job, not an obligation or responsibility; it's more like a fun hobby that happens to earn you money. The more you enjoy working on building a passive income, the more you'll succeed at creating something special that will attract consumers.

Although we are going to suggest ten sources that others have found to be profitable and exciting, your sources of passive income are only limited by the bounds of your creativity. This chapter will introduce you to some tried and proven streams of passive income. In the chapters to follow, we will go into depth on how to begin building each one of these sources. The exciting thing about passive income is that you get to take a source, explore and expand all the possibilities of turning that source into a stream of revenue, and discover how you can motivate and inspire others to join in, participating in the adventure because they believe in you and your offering.

The following ten sources of passive income have helped many beginners build their financial futures, but it does come at a cost. Typically, the more money you invest, the less time it requires to maintain the stream. However, many of the suggested sources don't require a great deal of monetary investment, so don't think you must have a sizeable nest egg before starting your stream of passive income. Be prepared, though, to spend your spare time away from the television and into ways you can generate avenues of income.

10 Sources of Passive Income

1. Writing eBooks

    You don't have to be an excellent writer to build a pipeline of eBooks that will earn you money while you move forward with other sources. All you need to do is find topics you know enough about to help or interest others. The great subject matter is key to success in eBooks. Once you have established topics you think readers would enjoy and benefit from; you're halfway there. We'll show you how to start a pipeline of eBooks without ever writing a word.

2. Developing Apps

    Again, you don't have to be an expert programmer to design and develop an incredible app that would be useful to others. As we go, we'll show you how you can hire the work done efficiently and competently, and get onto making money. We'll teach you how to identify a problem and create a solution with your app. You'll learn how to design and market your app so that users will be eager to see what's coming next. It won't just stop with one app. Once you learn the process, you'll begin to think like a real problem solver. Soon, you'll be an expert at discovering and designing apps that help people in their day-to-day lives. Creating passive income through the development of apps can be a rewarding endeavor—both financially and emotionally!

3. Creating Blogs

When you are building your sources of passive income, you'll want to do so with things in which you are already familiar. Don't worry if you are not yet an expert, once you've completed your research and discovery, you can tap into all the experts' information and learn to organize it in a way that is unique, interesting, and easy for consumers to follow. Highly intelligent people are not experts at everything, they simply know how to surround themselves with other very smart individuals who are experts, and then they tap into that expert knowledge and skill to build their own success.

Blogs are a way to create a following where readers recognize the value of the information you impart. Think of blogs as a vehicle in which to deliver information and inspire people to continue to learn more about the topic you have chosen. You're the teacher, gathering eager students whose goal is to absorb all your knowledge and skills and apply your expertise.

4. Developing Websites

   Again, don't worry about not knowing how to write code or develop a website. You just need to be the idea person. Yours is to create and inspire; let others who are expert web developers activate your ideas. We'll show you in a later chapter all the amazing things you can do with a website that works while you're not.

5. Investing in Stocks

   Some people think they must have a lot of money and knowledge to invest in stocks. That's a myth. Remember what I said about starting small and then letting your investments work for you. When you invest a little, chances are you're not going to make an overnight killing on a magical rise in your stock's value. You'll invest a little, and you'll make a little, and then you'll reinvest a little more until you build up that nest egg. Keep your energy invested in the journey, and for the moment, don't worry about the end destination.

6. Investing in Bonds

Investing in bonds is a long-term endeavor. Although this is almost the purest form of passive income, it is also one in which your mindset must be about "future" financial freedom. Bonds are slow growing but typically very steady and reliable.

7. Buying Annuities

Buying annuities can be tricky. As we

introduce this source of income, we'll give you tips on what to buy and what to avoid. We'll discuss the pros and cons of buying annuities so that you can decide whether this source of passive income is right for you.

8. Creating Rental Income

    Many people believe this source of passive income requires $25,000 or more to purchase a rental property, but we'll teach you how to build a rental income with minimal investments of time and money. This is a source that is wide open for innovative thinkers. Rental opportunities are typically growing investments with excellent returns. Notice I didn't say stable? There's no such thing as stable when it comes to passive income. If your source is stable, you're losing money.

9. Buying Mortgages

Think of these as paper exchanges. You can buy others' mortgages or even become a private lender. This source of passive income can be quite profitable and require little time, but you will need to have some financial backing to begin. This may be one that you'll want to start after you've had some success with your other sources.

10. Product Development and Resale

Anybody can do this, and it can be a lot of fun. We'll show you how the experts have learned to buy low and sell high. You'll learn to recognize the right products, maintain the proper working inventory, and track your success. Keep your eyes and ears open, and you might also invent a whole new product or service that excites consumers enough to follow you and see what spinoffs may occur.

Using several of these sources, and perhaps more that you find particularly interesting will prepare you for incredible success in building a productive stream of passive income. The reason we suggest many sources, and a variety of ways to use those sources, is because the more sources used, the greater chance you have for success. If one source in the stream fails to produce, go to another. If one source does well for you and then slows to a crawl, it will give you time to focus on other things. Rarely does passive income stream steady, so you ride one while you continue to develop another and another.

That's what makes passive income so different from a regular 9-5 job; you're not stuck in one field or industry. Instead, you can explore and expand your thinking; creativity is the name of the game. Your innovations can be richly rewarding. Instead of being frustrated by short-sighted, status quo superiors who cannot appreciate maverick thinkers like you, you'll find great satisfaction in coming up with new sources of passive income and exciting ways to make those sources work for you.

Remember, you are erecting a platform from which to launch your passive income portfolio. The more sources used, the greater the stream of passive income you will create. Hanging in there for long-term profits is key. Beginning small and building is smart. Creating sources of income with a visionary plan will prepare you for the challenges, setbacks, and successes you will experience along the way. The journey can be bumpy and sometimes the mountain of issues you must overcome can seem insurmountable. If creating passive income happened by the snap of your fingers, there would be so many others out there doing it that the competition would kill your efforts.

This is the perfect time to discuss the advantages of embracing that competitive spirit. We're not talking about the kind of competition that creates bitter rivalries that destroy or cripple one's ability to succeed. That kind of competitive spirit serves no one. However, there is a competition that teaches and inspires you to become better, to learn from others mistakes, and to help you decide how you plan to separate yourself from the pack and provide a unique product or service. So, let's examine the benefits of embracing your competition.

Five Main Benefits of Embracing Your Competition

1. Competition can create in you desire to become the best.

> Musicians having to compete for fans have created some of their most artistic work in their attempts to be better than the rest. Inventors become more innovative problem solvers when they have fierce competition. Technological engineers become more insightful to the needs of the public when their competition comes knocking at their doors. People who desire to become the best often push themselves to peak performance.

2. Make additional discoveries in the competitive journey.

> Because you are studying your competition to become the best, you will learn a great deal of how and why they do things the way they do.

You'll also discover what NOT to do, and change the things you don't like into strategies that will help you become successful. Knowing what others are doing will enable you to engage with the consumers in a different way—in a way that makes your offering unique and allows you to stand out from the crowd.

3. Embracing your competition can save you money and time.

It's so much easier to learn from someone else's mistakes. There have been many times that I have saved myself money and time by learning what my competition was doing well, adopting those strategies, and then improving on them to do an even better job. Embracing and studying my competition taught me how to work smarter and leaner. Since time means money, any time that can be saved in your startup is of significant value.

4. Competition encourages you to be more creative.

You can get a lot of ideas from your competition and modify them to suit the way you prefer to do business. Or, you can just study what doesn't work, why consumers need something new and different, and then create that opportunity for them to shop in a broader marketplace.

5. Most of all, competition creates a need for innovative and ongoing change. Someone else will come in and do something that is different and better, then you adopt that strategy and

move forward to improve on it and develop something else different and better. It's ongoing—good for consumers and good for business.

To become successful in creating a good stream of passive income you've got to do two things: a) show consumers why they need what you are offering; and, b) explain why you should be the one to provide that particular product or service. Sounds easy—but it requires thought, planning, time, and money.

CHAPTER 2: A PIPELINE OF E-BOOKS, APPS, AND BLOGS

Creating passive income from these three sources can be labor intensive, or they can be a wonderful outlet for your creative genius. Once you have put the upfront work in, the profits are almost 100%. With very little maintenance and no labor-intensive inventory to worry about, you can begin making money in a matter of weeks. Building a pipeline of e-Books, apps, and blogs can help you to bring in immediate passive income, and you can then take some of that profit to invest in other things.

Why Are e-Books a Good Source of Passive Income

Before you turn off to this subject because you think you don't have the talent to write a book, think again. Remember, you don't have to do the actual writing; you can hire that done by a professional writer. These writers can be found in a variety of places online for a very affordable price. Sites like www.eWriterSolutions.com, www.upworks.com, or www.outsource.com are just a few sources where you can find excellent writers. Why belabor the writing, when for under $250 you can have your book done in a matter of weeks?

Creating a pipeline of eBooks can give you so much flexibility in your work. You can live anywhere that has a high-speed internet connection for your computer and beach-front Margarita's for your celebration when the book has been completed. Because e-Books are digital, you don't have to worry about the cost of print, to lease a warehouse to store inventory, or hiring employees to fulfill orders. We'll discuss later how easy it is to get your book into the hands of consumers.

Even though the information you have provided in your book may be available in other locations, you've taken the time and trouble to gather it all in one book, while putting your own unique twist on the topic. Once you begin writing e-Books, you will soon become the recognized expert. Link your e-Books to a regular blog posting and a website, and you have instant marketing avenues.

The other great thing about writing e-Books is that they have a constant demand, especially if you've learned how to maintain their popularity through effective marketing strategies. This example of the amount of passive income that could be generated with e-Books will excite you. Let's say you had ten e-Books in your passive income pipeline. Now let's estimate a conservative shelf-life of twelve months for each book, and we'll set the price at $5 per book. Let's say you had interesting topics and were selling on average of 10 copies per book per day. Your six-month passive income for all ten books would be $18,250 per year.

Okay, now let's pretend you came up with great topics but did not feel comfortable in writing them yourself, so to hire a professional your writing fees would be $200 per book. Ten books at $200 would cost you a total of $2,000. There are also places online to find a designer to create a great cover for your book. Again, it may cost you $200 per book to have it done, so that would be another $2,000 for all ten books. Taking your writing and design expenses from the $18,250 would leave you $14,250. If you choose to market your books on Amazon, it will usually cost you approximately 30% of the price of the book, which in this case would be $5,475, leaving you $8,775.

Keep in mind, the more e-Books you write, the better you market them, and the longer shelf life they have will just increase the passive income you can expect to make. Starting with only one book is fine, and you can let the proceeds you make from that one help you to pay for the next. Starting small is the way to go. However, you cannot stop after you have written just one, you'll need to keep feeding your pipeline, so the income continues.

You can also use a service like Lulu that will take your uploaded e-Book and place it on multiple platforms for you, instead of you going to each site to upload. Of course, there is an additional charge for that, which is usually another percent or two of the price of your book. To use this service, simply go to https://www.lulu.com, set up your account, and upload your book (2).

If you fancy yourself a writer and plan on using this source extensively to earn passive income, you can also start a blog and website to promote your work. And, if you want to do all your own marketing and fulfillment, you'll keep almost 100% of the profits. Of course, it means more time invested, so weigh all the pros and cons of doing so. The beauty of having Amazon handle everything for you is that you won't have to keep accounts, manage payments, handle distribution, refunds, or returns. You should be able to rely on the platforms you use to provide excellent service. They should also have such a huge market, that it makes the job of promoting your books much easier because you will have a broad base of customers. That's why you pay them 30% of your profits.

With all these resources and tools, all you do is come up with exciting and interesting topics. Try to write about topics that are popular, reach a broad customer base, and that aren't already flooding the market. Although that won't even be a concern if your e-Books contain exceptional information and are well written.

Creating an App as Passive Income

Just like the writing process, you don't have to become a professional coder or programmer to create an incredible app. All the development can be done at an affordable price by the experts. Of course, if you want to take the time to learn to code, you can, but this is time spent that could be better used developing more sources of passive income, don't you think? If you are excited about being the idea man or woman and leaving the labor to those who know how to provide you with an incredible product, then let's move forward, shall we?

One of the most frequently asked questions most people have when developing their first app is—how do I know what kind of app to create? Where do I begin? Here are five easy steps to follow that will help you to decide.

1. Consider a skill or talent you have in which

you and others believe to be your particular area of expertise. Perhaps it is a past career, a hobby, or a creative outlet in which you excel. If you can think of nothing you have done where you stood out from the crowd, then think of something that is fascinating to you and perhaps will also be to a wide range of other people.

2. As you consider your area of expertise, think about a specific problem you had when you were first learning to perform this skill or job. For example, let's say you love to garden and have a talent for growing beautiful vegetables —but, this has not always been the case. Let's say it took you a long time to learn about what soil, seasons, temperatures and sunlight requirements were needed for the many vegetables you were interested in cultivating.

Through many trials and errors, much research and failed attempts, you finally have a productive vegetable garden that consistently raises bumper crops. You could design a handy app to resolve the initial issues that you experienced, so that consumers would only be a click away in determining what vegetable to plant where, when.

3. Now that you have thought of what you want your app to about ask yourself how you can create that app to resolve some of the problems you first experienced. How can you help consumers to achieve greater success investing less time and money?

4. Don't rely entirely on yourself when identifying a problem and solution, especially

if you are not an expert in your field of interest. Find people who are currently working in your area of interest or enjoying your hobby and ask lots of questions. Then interview experts to see how they suggest these issues could be resolved. Now, you have the makings of an app.

5. If you simply cannot think of anything, identify some of the day-to-day, repetitive tasks people do that could be achieved more efficiently if they could just click for information. Apps typically provide excellent solutions for repetitive tasks that many people do on a daily basis.

Now you need to focus on how you plan to market and sell your app. Like e-Books, you can sell your app over the Internet by using platforms such as www.e-junkie or www.gumroad.com. Or, you can sell your app on a third-party marketplace like Win 8App Store or Mac App Store. The advantages of using Microsoft or Apple is that they have massive search engines and amazing delivery systems in place. The only way anybody makes money is when your app sells, so everybody works hard to make sure your app is a success (3).

Similar to Amazon for your e-Books, Apple takes about a 30% cut to bring your app to the consumer. They have certain guidelines you must go through for approval, and, of course, there are many apps available, so the competition is high. However, many app developers have not done near the homework or have near the expertise to back up the function of their apps, right? All the support and visibility Apple can provide will more than makes up for the 30% charge.

Blogging is a Beautiful Thing—Six Steps to Success

Starting a blog doesn't have to be rocket science, but your first time out of the gate can be intimidating, especially if you're not a computer whiz. The following are six easy steps to practice that will help you create an incredible blog and maximize the potential passive income you can generate.

Step #1: Ask yourself why you want to start a blog.

I hope your only answer to this question isn't just to make money. Although it's an excellent way to create passive income, if money is your only reason, you're setting yourself up for failure. Blogs that are started because someone wants to make a difference, to become a better person, or to get published, are going to be ones that attract a bigger following. Unless you are blogging about ways to increase your income—like generating passive income—talking about income made from your blog won't be terribly impressive.

Step #2: What will be the focus of your blog?

What are your hobbies, talents, and things in which you are passionate? When you're with a group of people, what do you find yourself talking about most of the time? That may be your first blog. Make sure the topic of your blog is broad enough to continue sharing information about it over an extended period.

Step #3: What blogging platforms do you plan to use?

There are many free hosting sites; however, since your blog is to promote whatever will create passive income for you, it is better to have a self-hosted WordPress blog. Besides, free blog sites aren't ever free because the myriad of limitations they place on you will inhibit your ability to reach maximum followers. What are the costs of a self-hosted blog? With many hosting accounts, you can get a domain name for free. The average fee for an account is approximate $75 for the first year.

Web Hosting Hub is reliable and affordable. They provide excellent customer support with 99.9% server uptime. They offer a free domain name, and their service is quite easy for beginners. They also offer unlimited bandwidth, disk space, and email accounts. If you are not satisfied, Web Hosting Hub offers a 90-day money back guarantee. If you decide blogging is not for you, you can simply cancel your account and ask for a refund.

Step #5: Create Your Blog

Since this is dependent on which host you chooses to use, the best thing to do is search online for the web host you desire and follow their step-by-step guidelines.

Step #6: Start Blogging

If you have chosen a reputable web host, it is as simple as logging in with your username and password and posting your first blog. Decide how often you wish to post a new blog, and let your readers know. Also, link your blog to your website and your e-Books. This will create excellent synergy for the promotion of all your sources of passive income. The best blogs are ones that are fun, informative, fun, creative, fun, theme based—oh, and did I mention fun (4)?

Whichever sources you decide to use, or if you incorporate all of them into your passive income portfolio, make it entertaining for your followers and yourself. If building passive income becomes a chore, you're not going to want to give up your free time and spare money to make it work. So, the best advice that I can give you is to choose sources of passive income that you will enjoy, and you think others will as well.

CHAPTER 3: REAL ESTATE RETURNS

Owning real estate rental property is a long-term investment. Although it is not as liquid as cash in hand or the bank, it can eventually net you quite a return, especially if you have positive cash flow from your rental. There are certain things to keep in mind when investing in rental property, and they are as follows:

10 Tips for Investing in Rental Property

1. The location is everything.

Make sure your location will support the rent amount needed to cover your mortgage. If not, you'll end up with a negative cash flow that will eat into your passive income. No matter how well-maintained the home or apartment building you are purchasing is, it's not going to be consistently rented if the surrounding neighborhood is dangerous or poorly kept—unless, of course, you plan on being a slum lord, and that's a whole other headache.

2. When investing, don't be shy about asking for the moon in your purchase contract.

The worse that could happen is that the owner will refuse your offer, and then you can counter in hopes of finding the best possible price. Before you begin the negotiations, decide on what your ceiling offer is, and stick to that figure. The price you pay for the property should be well below the appraised value so that you can start as a landlord in an equal position.

Include, in writing, any additional appliances, fans, and window coverings you want to go with the sale. Also, be aware of other costs that will need to be paid upfront, such as HOA transfer fees and appraisal fees. Because these fees must be paid before the property closes, you don't want to get stuck with these out-of-pocket costs should the property not close. A good practice in these situations is to negotiate that the owner pays these costs and closing costs if possible. If the owner insists on splitting these fees, then negotiate that the owner pays up front and be reimbursed as closing. That way, if the property doesn't close, you won't be out the money.

Since you want to invest as little upfront money as possible, negotiate everything that you can to be put into the mortgage. For example, raise the price of the property and have the owner pay for the closing costs; this will enable you to purchase with no upfront closing costs. Your closing costs will be wrapped into your mortgage. Look for properties that have been on the market for some time, since the owners will be more open to negotiating price or perks. NEVER, EVER purchase property without doing a thorough inspection by a paid professional. When repairs need to be made, either has the repairs completed before closing or ask that the owners renegotiate their asking price.

If the property already has a tenant, realize that you will most likely need to give them a 30-day notice or honor the existing lease agreement. Ask the owners to review the existing rental agreement to see what your obligations are regarding the current tenant. Make sure you have also done an excellent job considering what rents are going for in that area, and see how those properties compare with the one you are interested in purchasing.

3.   The best investment isn't always the prettiest property.

Keep in mind; this is to be a rental property—not one in which you are planning to live. Any improvements made should be practical and economical, not necessarily the most expensive and luxurious. It is usually not a good idea to have a lot of extras on a rental, like a pool or a fireplace, for instance. They create additional liabilities, and the cost of maintenance or upkeep cannot be recouped in rental fees.

4. Be prepared for repairs after each vacating tenant.

Tenants are going to damage your property, and you

need to be prepared, so you are not blindsided by costly repairs. It's important that you require regular inspections of the property, done by yourself or your management company. If you see that the property is neglected or abused, give your immediate tenant notice to vacate before you lose money and valuable time making unnecessary repairs. Even though having a management company will cost you a little money upfront, they can save you so much in the long run. Not only will they save you money, but if you actually want passive income from your rentals, then you need to distance yourself from the day-to-day hassles of rental management.

5. Increase rental incomes for long-term tenants.

The mistake many investors make is that they fail to raise rents for long-term tenants. Your leases should have potential built-in rate increases that are written into the lease agreements. If you have an excellent tenant, then you'll want to reward them by maintaining a reasonable rental fee. However, that doesn't mean raising the rent. If your tenant has been in the property for a long time, you will still be expected to paint and replace flooring from time to time, and your rental fees will need to cover those costs. Set aside enough positive cash flow to cover repairs and updates to your rental. This will keep it market fresh and make it more appealing to a wide range of potential tenants.

6. Plan on regular tax increases and elevated HOA fees.

Before purchasing your property review what the taxes and HOA fees have done over the past five years. Were the taxes steady, or have they increased substantially? Look at the amount they have increased over this period, and plan on that continuing. The same can be said for HOA fees. First of all, make sure you have included HOA fees in your rental fees because you will be responsible for paying them—not the tenant. You don't want to have taxes and HOA fees eat up your passive income from the property, so those costs should be figured into your rentals.

7. Keep as much money in your pocket as possible.

There are many ways to purchase property that won't cost you an arm and a leg for a down payment and closing costs. In fact, you can buy cooperatively with other investors for as little as $5,000, and enjoy all the benefits of passive income in your rental. If you decide on this method of investing in real estate, make sure you have spelled out in your agreement the requirements of selling your portion of the property. The downside to these types of investments is that it can often be harder to sell your ownership share.

If you decided that shared real estate investment is a way for you to get your foot in the door, one such company to check into is RealtyShares. RealtyShares is one of the largest real estate crowdsourcing companies, and it is based in San Francisco. They include a variety of nationwide investment opportunities in both residential and commercial properties. This can be quite advantageous as you can pick and choose locations around the country, purchasing when the markets are at their best (5).

8. Don't outstay your welcome in a rental

investment.

What I mean by that is that every property has a predetermined useful life. Don't keep the property beyond its earning potential. If the repairs you are consistently making outweigh the return, it may be time to sell and reinvest in another rental. Track your appreciation to determine whether your money would earn you more in a different area of property. In most markets and locations, the life of a property is, at its maximum, no longer than 29 years. The life of a property is dependent upon its age at purchase, and whether it is residential or commercial. Some commercial property has a longer life than residential.

9. You can also trade properties of like type and value.

There are tax requirements to consider when

trading properties, and a professional can help you with this. However, this can be an excellent way to gain instant equity in a property, since the trade does not have term requirements, but only refers to the purchase price. For example, if you have a property that has no equity but is in a great location, and you want cash to invest in additional passive income opportunities, you could trade with someone who does have equity. After the trade, you could then pull some of the equity from your newly acquired property to invest in several others without any out-of-pocket costs.

10. You can also purchase paper (privately held notes or deeds) on a property.

This usually requires more money, but there is no maintenance or upkeep—you are only purchasing the paper. You don't own the property, unless, of course, the payee should default—which would mean you own the entire property for a fraction of the price. When you purchase paper, you own the paper or the loan. For example, let's say the original owner sold the home that he owned free and clear and created a private mortgage or loan on the property for the buyers. Each month, the buyer makes a payment of $1,000 to the original owner. Because the original owner was willing to carry the financing, he receives significantly more interest on his money—let's say 10%. The remainder owed on loan is $50,000 at 10% interest.

For personal reasons, the original owner decides he needs cash and wants to sell the private note he is carrying at a substantial discount. It is feasible that you could purchase a $50,000 note for $30,000 and make 10% interest on your investment. You will still have to honor the terms of the original loan, but you have just made $20,000, and you will earn a good deal more money on your investment. Of course, you too have the option to sell the paper to another investor like yourself who is also interested in purchasing the paper.

Don't worry about the chances of the buyers defaulting because that is not a bad thing for your investment. If they default, then you are the owner of the property. The more equity in the property, the better. In fact, a good rule of thumb when investing in the paper is that there should be at least 10% equity in the property. More equity is always better, but 10% equity is a must.

There are so many different opportunities to make passive income in real estate investments; whatever you can imagine can usually be created in a purchase agreement. Just be careful that you have done your homework and that you are not buying something with an inflated price or unreasonable terms. If you find that real estate is your primary source of passive income, you may want to consider obtaining a real estate license so you can save yourself the commissions on the property you sell and get paid the commissions on ones you purchase. That's a whole other source of passive income. It doesn't require any more work than your original purchase, and you'll be putting commissions in your pocket.

CHAPTER 4: INVESTING IN STOCKS, BONDS & ANNUITIES

Investing in stocks, bonds, and annuities can mean a chunk of change, so you may want to start out smaller and work your way up to this type of passive income. Let your money work for you on your other ventures and then use those profits to invest in stocks, bonds, and annuities. You can also make interest off CDs held in the bank, but today's rates are so low it won't gain you much income. There are different ways to invest in stocks, but if you are unfamiliar with the market the best way is to hire a reputable broker.

The safest way to invest your money is to do so with stable, reliable companies. Your returns won't be huge, but, as I said before, passive income is not a get-rich-quick scheme. You've got time, so it's probably better to play it safe and let your passive income gradually build. Of course, you're not always going to come out a winner, so if you're the anxious type who watches his or her money fluctuate each day and gets stressed with the roller-coaster ride of trading stocks, then this is not the best option for you.

If you decide to give it a try, develop a relationship with a good broker. Communicate your goals to your broker and trust them to help you choose which stocks to invest in and what is better left to the high-risk players. There are also stock options you can consider, but those are beyond the scope of this book. It will take some research for you to decide which stock to purchase and how many shares. If you are interested, the best thing is to research, study the market for a while before investing, and then pick a few favorites to watch for a while before you lay down the cash.

Diversify your stocks so that if one is down perhaps the others will be on the rise. Don't invest more than you can afford to lose. Investing in dividend-bearing stocks is an excellent way to draw money on your investment without selling the stock periodically. Choosing stable, reliable companies will enable you to collect regularly paid dividends and still leave your investment and let it continue to create more passive income. By choosing well, diversifying your portfolio, and investing several thousand dollars in dividend-based stock, you stand to make four to five percent on your investment without selling. It's passive but, don't kid yourself; it can be quite stressful.

If you're planning the DIY type of stock investing, let us warn you that the learning curve can be very expensive. Years ago, a close friend of my family decided to spend her $35,000 inheritance in the stock market. She thought it would be fun to become a day trader and work from home, and felt her inheritance would give her a good start. She read up and studied the market for months before finally quitting her job and buying her stock. Within a matter of six months, she had lost all her money and was out looking for another job. Although day trading can sound like a lot of fun, it requires knowledge and nerves of steel to hang in there through the ups and downs of the market.

One of the best investments for a novice trader is Exchange-Traded Funds (ETFs). These are investments that have assets such as stocks, bonds, and commodities; however, they are easier to understand and much more liquid. They also come with a lower price tag than investing in mutual funds. ETFs are especially rewarding for the young investor who doesn't have much money to spend so he or she would be unable to make a broker's deposit of $5,000 to $10,000, but they would enjoy a higher-risk stock. ETFs could either be included in their portfolio, or the trader could invest in ETFs entirely. It is still required, however, to pay a broker's fee on every ETF transaction (6).

Investing in Bonds and Bank Savings

These are probably the safest investment, and yet your gains will be minimal. If you have waited until you are retired to begin building passive income, these are not going to mature quickly enough to make a difference. They are such a solid investment, and you can count on them to grow to match inflation, but not much more. The biggest risk made when investing in bonds is that you have left money on the table by not putting your money somewhere else that could have grown faster and significantly increased your passive income.

There are short-term and long-term bonds with differing maturity dates. Think of bonds like a loan and the maturity date as the time in which the bond issuer is required to pay you back the entire loan amount. The longer the term to maturity, the more time you'll have to collect interest on the bond. The benefit to you for lending the money is that you get to collect interest on the bond, and at the time of maturity, you get back your initial investment. The only time you would not get your investment back is if the issuer has defaulted or you sell the bond to another investor before its maturity.

If you want to avoid broker fees, you can purchase bonds directly from the Treasure. Just visit their online site at http://www.treasurydirect.gov, and everything will be handled electronically. If you are using a broker and have decided to include bonds in your portfolio, you will then pay a broker's fee. Most brokers will ask for a minimum deposit of $5,000 to $10,000 to open your account and invest your money, so be prepared (7).

Bank CDs are less of a risk than bonds, but they also provide fewer returns. The beauty of CDs is that they are liquid (easily converted to cash) should you need your money in a hurry. The problem with CDs in today's market is their interest is so low; your money is better spent in another passive source. The interest on a CD depends on how much you put into the CD and how long you plan to leave it there. You can put thousands into a CD and commit to leaving it there for years and still get no more than 1 or 2 percent return. No risk—no return. It would probably cost you more in gas to pick up your money.

Investing in Annuities

Annuities are typically purchased from an insurance company. You buy the policy and then it pays you a specified amount each year for the rest of your life. The younger you are when you invest in the annuity, the less it will pay you each year. The dangers with annuities are that the insurance company might go belly-up and leave you holding the bag. For this reason, choose insurance companies that have been around for years and have proven themselves in the marketplace. You also may wish to diversify when investing in annuities, spreading your money with several insurance companies.

Annuities can also be inherited, but make sure you communicate to your beneficiary any annuity you may have. Insurance companies are not held liable to inform recipients that their deceased donor had an annuity that was willed to them and they are now the recipient of thousands of dollars. Don't hold your breath on that happening! If your chosen beneficiary doesn't know to call and notify the insurance company of the change in name or status of the annuity, they might not ever collect. By the time your intended beneficiary got around to discovering you willed your annuity to them, the insurance company may well have eaten up the profits in service fees (8).

If you are a bit intimidated with the thought of investing in stocks and annuities, that's understandable. Starting small is difficult with these types of investments, especially if your broker requires large deposits. Some brokerage houses will allow novice investors to begin with minimum deposits of a few thousand dollars, and some offer you investment money to sign up with their investment firm. A word of caution, be careful when going with brokers who entice with free offers. There might be a good reason they feel as though they must pay for their clients.

Investing in the market is not for the faint of heart. So, if you don't do stress—don't invest, especially if you are investing money that you would lose sleep over if you lost it tomorrow. Stick to other ways to create passive income that won't give you heartburn if you should drop a few thousand during your learning curve. For some, that could be all the money they have saved or earned by their entire stream of passive income. Don't risk it all—instead, start small!

CHAPTER 5: BUILDING/BUYING WEBSITES & DOMAINS

There is a whole new world of online commerce out

there in the form of websites and domains. You can build them, buy them, or flip them, but whatever you do will mean some upfront investment of time and money. Of course, you can always think of a domain name, register it, and use or sell it. You can do the same with a website—build it or pay for it to be built, then use it to promote your stream of passive income. Sounds good, but those of you who have ever attempted to have experts create a website for you know the expense and frustration that can cause. The DIY job of building a website doesn't get you the optimization you'll need to put your business on the map. So, what do you do?

The first website I built was through GoDaddy. While it looked good, it was not successful at driving browsers to my site. I knew nothing of keywords, WordPress, reviews, ads, links, nothing—and so that is what the website was worth to my business—

absolutely nothing. Then I met with an SEO and paid to have the website optimized. Eight-hundred dollars later, I still had an attractive website, and I believed the SEO was working on my behalf to make the site more functional, but, to tell you the truth, after months of asking where we were at with the optimization, I still had a whole lot of nothing. No more responses, very little traffic, and an empty purse.

Next, I hired a professional design company to give me a fresh start and create a whole new website for my business. This time I paid $16,000, and it looked outstanding. It was highly functioning, did exactly what I wanted it to do, drove business to the site, but there was one problem. I could not maintain the site myself. About once a week I had a challenge on the site that needed attention, and there I was— dependent upon the web designers to change the code and make the site work more efficiently. So now, not only was it highly expensive, it was extremely time-consuming. I ended up selling the business after 18 months. It was profitable, and the woman who purchased my business also owns the website. It was still a startup with existing contracts of over $60,000. The company sold for $32,000, which was barely enough to cover my cost of developing and maintaining the website during those miserable 18 months.

Who reaped the benefits of my website business? The person who purchased it; she didn't have to go through the months of frustrating design and content development or the initial start-up hassles for website maintenance and support. Since this was years ago, I didn't know about website sales, and they might not have even existed back then. I didn't sell my site; I sold my business. The problem was, I didn't think of my website as my business; I thought of it as a way to market my business.

The reason I share this story is that I wanted to give you a better perspective on how to think of a website. When I refer to selling websites, what I'm talking about is selling businesses. There are many sites online that have listings of website businesses for sale. They range from $50 on up to $15,000 or more. Sometimes the better bargain is not to build your site from scratch, but to buy a bargain business and let it provide immediate passive income.

There will always be the high-priced website companies that you pass by because you think they are cost prohibitive, but stop for a moment and give it a second look. If it is already making a sizeable passive income, you may want to take on a partner and do a little coop investing. Then there are the budget website businesses that you, again, pass by because you believe they couldn't be worth the hosting fees, right? Not necessarily. Look again. If the website is of interest to you, examine it to see how you could ramp up the site and generate new business. If all you save is the cost of website design, that, in itself, could mean thousands of dollars in your pocket.

Then there are the website businesses that are not too flashy, but they consistently perform. For most of you first-time website buyers, this will be the place to start to build up your site passive income (9). If your talent lies in writing code or programming, what are you thinking? Start building businesses around a website and then sell it, for goodness sake! Or, partner with a content writer, and together create some unusual sources for making passive income.

A real inexpensive way to build passive income is by buying domain names. They are inexpensive and, if you've done your homework, can be sold for incredible profits. Let me give you five easy to remember tips on what not to do when you're planning to buy and sell domain names.

5 Easy Tips on What Not to Do When Buying Domains

1. Don't cruise lots of sites looking for domain names, or versions of the domain names you like, to see if they are taken. Decide where you want to purchase your domain, and stick to that sight. Most domain names cost $10. If you find the domain is available, buy it

immediately. Don't wait until after dinner because, if it's a hot name that just happened to become available, it will be taken by then.

2. Don't ask other people what they think of your domain name. It might give them the idea to buy it from you and then sell back to you for a profit.

3. Don't buy just one version of the same domain. They are only $10, buy up the .net, .com, .org, .biz, all of them. What do you think another who likes your name will do when they see the domain is taken and not for sale? They will usually go to another version of the same name. For example, if .com is taken, they'll choose .net. If you own all the versions of the same domain, you can sell the .com version to them for a sizeable profit.

4. Don't buy a lot of domain names that you just think are cool. Look to see what the latest trends are in business. New business start-ups are public record, and corporations must publish their openings in the paper. Search to find what types of businesses are popular and then put yourself in the place of the owner. What names might relate to those kinds of businesses? Then, simply buy the domains.

5. Don't feel like you can't ask for a lot of money because you only paid $10 for the domain. Many rookie business owners fail to set up their businesses correctly, and that includes registering their names. By the time they get around to doing so, their preferred name is taken, and they are then required to pay

much, much more for the domain name. You were the visionary, and you should reap the benefits.

Finding places to buy and sell websites and domains are just a matter of a little online research. Many sites will lead you to these wonderful little gold mines of passive income.

CHAPTER 6: MONITOR & ADJUST YOUR SOURCES

Even though all these sources for passive income eventually take very little time, you still need to monitor the results of your investments and make the necessary adjustments for them to continue to run smoothly. If you're writing eBooks and creating apps, you need to keep your pipeline filled with current books and apps continually. If you are purchasing a rental property, you'll need to continuously search the market for bargains and determine which of your current assets are ready to be sold. If you are buying and selling websites and domains, it's a constant search for good little businesses and names. Think of yourself as the CEO of your passive income business. You don't have to do the grunt labor, just show up now and then.

Now you know why I said in the very beginning that it takes a lot of creativity and innovative thinking to create viable passive income. Don't turn this endeavor into a job, keep it adventurous. This is your chance to be an entrepreneur, to discover all the many ways or different businesses you can create that take little to no startup cost with a minimal amount of time spent in maintaining their ongoing profits.

I will tell you; it will be quite tempting to spend your

passive income when you see it begin to roll in but resist. Celebrate just a little, briefly indulge yourself, then set aside some money for more investments and always save. I've found that when you have passive income and things get tough, everything comes crashing down at once. It can be very discouraging, and many who made a good start on building passive income quit during the first storm because they weren't prepared to ride it out—both financially and emotionally.

By monitoring and adjusting what works and what doesn't work, your stream will stay active and your passive income consistent. Frequently examine the cost, in time and money, to maintain your sources of passive income. If one source of passive income costs you more time than you want to devote to it, drop it. That's not failing; it's called smart business practices. Some sources you don't have to drop; just let them ride away into the sunset until they dry up and stop producing altogether. However, there are other things you will need to shut down, or the small strings of business will make you crazy to maintain them. It will be too much work for too little returns.

Always search for new sources of passive income. What you think are great sources today will become obsolete tomorrow. It's an ever-changing ocean of newness; to be most successful you must surf the curl or be buried by the waves of change. Stay current with technology, and learn how to make it work for you. Technology an excellent tool, even if used only to track your successes and setbacks. Make technology your business partner; in doing so, you can often create new business in a matter of days and change existing ones at the click of a key.

This doesn't have to be a business of one. In some

of my businesses, I've taken on partners who were more technically savvy than me, or who were experts in the field in which I wished to learn more. That doesn't mean you should partner in every source of your passive income, but in some avenues having a partner enables you to make more money in less time. If you do take on a partner, make sure you have clearly communicated your expectations and put everything in writing.

Most importantly, and I cannot emphasize this enough, make it FUN! Build passive income by doing the things you've always wanted to do, by creating unique and entertaining profitable avenues of revenue. It is so much easier to market businesses that you believe in and enjoys. It's just natural to want to talk to your friends about what you're doing when you love your work.

I've heard it said that work should fund your life but not be your life. I'm not so sure this is the case with passive income. What you enjoy most in life soon becomes the work that you enjoy most. I love my work so much; it's difficult for me to separate the two at times. I can't imagine going on vacation and not thinking about what my sources of passive income are doing while I'm away. Most people think of their pets having a field day while they are away, but those of us who love creating passive income have better things on which to focus. We know the importance of keeping our creative juices flowing all the time. Think of your passive income as a game—a game where you get to make the rules and determine the outcomes.

Be prepared for some ups and downs, especially

when you first begin building your stream. If you're going to ride the rapids, you'll have to learn to navigate the rocky patches without drowning. It's an important time to share with a loved one or close friend what you are planning to do—someone who will encourage you—someone, with whom you can celebrate your successes. Choose these people carefully because, in the beginning, stage of your new passive income career, they may be the determining factor of whether you hang in there or drop out. Good luck with your efforts. Keep me posted; I'll love to share in all your victories.

THANK YOU

Dear treasured reader, I would like to thank you from the bottom of my heart for choosing to purchase this book. I hope this book will help you select and develop a stream of passive income that will give you financial freedom. The next step is to jump right in and begin creating sources for your stream of passive income. Choose those you enjoy—those that will be exciting and create enthusiasm for you and others.

I hope you've gotten some valuable information that you can use daily to better your life and those around you as well. If you liked it would you be so kind as to leave an honest/positive review for my book. I would appreciate it very much.

To Your Success,
Jonathan S. Walker

www.ingramcontent.com/pod-product-compliance
Lightning Source LLC
LaVergne TN
LVHW010403070526
838199LV00065B/5885